Literacy Matters

Strategies Every Teacher Can Use

Robin Fogarty

PEARSON
SkyLight

Glenview, Illinois

Literacy Matters: Strategies Every Teacher Can Use

Published by Pearson Professional Development
1900 E. Lake Ave., Glenview, IL 60025
800-348-4474 or 847-657-7450
Fax 847-486-3183
info@pearsonpd.com
http://www.pearsonpd.com

LCCN 00-107314
ISBN 1-57517-361-1

2792-McN

Z Y X W V U T S R Q P O N M L K J I H G F E D
08 07 06 05 04   15 14 13 12 11 10 9 8 7 6 5

Dedication

To the science teacher,
the math teacher,
the social studies teacher,
the art, music, P.E., and special-needs teacher,
for each is, also,
the reading teacher.

—ROBIN FOGARTY

Acknowledgments

I want to acknowledge two people who have had significant impact on my thinking about the meaning of reading and about "literacy matters" in general: Chris Rauscher and Nelda Hobbs. Both helped me immensely with their feedback on the manuscript for *Literacy Matters,* but more importantly, with their fellowship as caring educators.

I remember as though it were yesterday, the question Chris Rauscher asked me, years ago, in Palatine, Illinois, School District #15, where she serves as Assistant Superintendent for Curriculum and Instruction. She said, simply, "What is reading?" In the simplicity of this question lies its complexity. What is reading? My answer: Reading is a window to the world. Of course, there are lots of other more technical answers, but that's the answer that makes the act of reading so compelling and so urgent an educational concern.

When I lamented to Nelda that I couldn't find a citation for the SQ3R strategy, she casually said, "It's Robinson." How did she know that off the top of her head? She knew that because she knows reading. After thirty plus years with the Chicago Public Schools, she knows this: If kids can't read, they can't do anything else. And she dedicates her work, in retirement, to helping teachers help kids to read.

Thanks to these two educators for their knowledge, expertise, and uncommon commitment to "literacy matters."

—ROBIN FOGARTY

Contents

Introduction

Two teachers are standing at their classroom doors across the hall from each other. They have just been to an early morning meeting about test scores . . .

Mr. Lou McGuire: If you can't read, you can't do much else in school. The fact that 30 percent of the children in our nation's schools can't read is astonishing to me.

Ms. Juanita Ramirez: Thirty percent? This is the most literate nation in the world. You must be confusing the data.

Mr. Lou McGuire: Somebody's confusing something, but it's not the data on literacy in our schools. According to an article I just read, researcher Bruce Joyce says, "About one-third of our students do not learn to read in the primary years, and very few of those students learn to read effectively later. The two-thirds who learn to read adequately in the early grades rarely reach their potential then or later" (Joyce 1999, 129). I think we're confused about our priorities.

Ms. Juanita Ramirez: I agree. A nation as wealthy as ours has no business neglecting the education of our children. If literacy truly was a national priority, all children would read and they would want to read, because they'd know they owned the key to lifelong literacy and learning.

Does this conversation sound familiar? What *can* teachers do? With *Literacy Matters,* teachers working with students across content areas as well as grade levels can promote literacy skills by using fifteen practical strategies. Each letter of *Literacy Matters* represents a strategy, as shown on page 8.

L earning to learn involves metacognition.

I nquiring readers comprehend more.

T apping into prior knowledge supports schema theory.

E xtensive reading encourages flexible reading.

R esearch on the brain informs educational practice.

A nalysis of words promotes reading proficiency.

C ooperative learning groups engage learners.

Y ou-are-a-reader attitude matters.

M ediate with early intervention strategies.

A ppealing to parents/guardians gets them involved.

T each vocabulary with key words.

T echnology impacts literacy.

E ntry points honor multiple intelligences.

R ead-aloud, read-along, read-appropriately practices
foster flexible reading.

S trategic reading is guided reading.

Literacy Matters defines each of these strategies and offers best practices teachers can use to help improve student literacy. The strategies not only cover the basic skills of literacy, but they also help students become aware of their literacy skill levels. *Literacy Matters* is a practical guide to enhancing literacy skills at any grade level and in any content area.

SkyLight Professional Development

Learning to Learn
Involves Metacognition

Learning how to learn is just as important as what one is learning—going beyond the cognitive and into the realm of the metacognitive. Metacognition is about planning, monitoring, and evaluating one's own thinking and learning. To illustrate the concept of metacognition, think about a student working a typical mathematics problem. The cognitive part of the lesson is the answer to the problem. The metacognitive part (Flavell 1979) is the student's awareness of the strategy he or she used to solve the problem and to arrive at the answer. When the teacher focuses the lesson on the strategy as well as the answer, the student thinks about how he or she solves problems and those strategies become part of the student's repertoire for future problems in mathematics as well as in other disciplines. By reflecting on the lesson, the student generalizes the learning and can apply it in diverse and novel situations.

Metacognition is about planning, monitoring, and evaluating . . .

Learning to learn, or metacognition, is about becoming aware of one's strengths and weaknesses as a learner. It is about acting on that awareness to change the way one does things. Once the learner is aware, that learner gains control over future learning situations. Teachers must explicitly weave metacognitive strategies into the fabric of the teaching-learning process. It is easily integrated into the thinking processes before, during, and after the lesson.

Best Practice Use Mediated Journals Before the Lesson

It is often appropriate to define terms prior to the lesson; therefore, an examination of the term literacy serves as a way to illustrate using metacognition before the lesson. Literacy is a robust concept that can be somewhat ambiguous. What is the definition of literacy as it applies to reading? To help develop a personal definition of literacy, try the following reflective strategy with students.

A mediated journal entry is an entry with prompts by the teacher that cue the student to respond. The prompts get the student thinking by "priming the pump." Using the concept of the mediated journal entry, have students respond to the following prompts to describe a literate person:

1. Name someone you believe is literate (personal acquaintance, celebrity, historical figure, or fictional character).
2. List two traits of the literate person you selected.
3. Describe someone who is not a literate person.
4. Tell how the two are different.
5. Write a summary sentence.
6. Title your piece: A Literate Person.

After completing the journal entry, think about the benefits of being a literate person and the repercussions of being nonliterate. Some issues might include self-esteem, school and grades, open doors, or the gatekeeper concept of "closed gateways" to higher education and other opportunities.

Use Literacy Ranking During the Lesson

During the lesson, teachers can further examine the elements of literacy by having students rank the four elements of literacy according to strengths: reading, writing, speaking, and listening. Students can then justify their rankings of literacy elements with further reflection (see Figure 1).

Return to Mediated Journals After the Lesson

Again, a proven tool for explicit attention to reflective learning following the learning is the mediated journal, which guides the student entry with lead-ins (Fogarty 1994). Lead-ins do just that. They lead the student to write a reflection. A lead-in leads students to think in critical and creative ways. Notice how the various lead-ins dictate a certain kind of thinking on the part of the student:

> I wonder . . .
> A conclusion I have drawn is . . .
> Comparing the two . . .
> What if . . . ?
> A problem I'm having is . . .
> The easiest part was . . .
> My worry is . . .
> How might I . . . ?

As students respond to the lead-ins, they begin to solidify their thinking about the learning and they begin to develop a keen awareness about how they learn. This kind of self-feedback is critical to the concepts of lifelong literacy and learning.

Literacy Ranking

Rank the elements of literacy according to your strengths:

_____Reading

_____Writing

_____Speaking

_____Listening

Think about how you might pursue your weaker areas or why you might not want to pursue them.

Figure 1

Reading, writing, speaking, and listening are inextricably linked in the journey toward becoming a literate person. Use the mediated journal as a literacy tool to prompt thinking prior to the lesson and again following the lesson as a review tool to deepen comprehension. Have students label various sections of the journal. Use labels such as the following:

- Vocabulary
- Summaries
- Characters to Remember
- Great Beginnings
- Literary Illuminations
- Write your Own Endings
- Kinds of Stories I Like

Discuss with students how these labels are not only helpful signals about the important information to capture when reading, but also they are helpful following the reading to capture the key points. Compare the mediated journal to typical text organizers such as headings, boldface type, and italics. Talk about how the text organizers and mediated entries act as signals to the reader or learner to pay closer attention.

▌ Inquiring Readers Comprehend More

An active reader is an inquiring reader. Inquiring readers carry on inner dialogues as they read:

- What is this all about?
- What is going on here?

- What is going to happen next?
- What does this really mean?

Skillful readers inquire about the mood, tone, setting, facts, descriptions, accuracy, assumptions, and biases of the author as they read between the lines. To read between the lines, readers go beyond the given information and make inferences about what is happening (Anderson et al. 1984). For example, when an author writes "The woman returned to the porch, drenched from head to foot," readers can infer that if the woman is drenched, readers realize that the woman is very wet. Then, readers think about how she became drenched and conclude it is probably raining. If the woman is drenched, it must be raining quite hard. Readers have to think and picture what the words are saying to understand what is happening. Readers have to question, wonder, and inquire as they read.

To encourage all readers to model what good readers do, teachers can use the read-think scenario.

To encourage all readers to model what good readers do, teachers can use the read-think scenario. The memory cue is read-think, read-think, read-think. That is the pattern of literacy, modeled by a good reader. The questioning cue is What am I thinking?–Why am I thinking that? These are the types of questions that foster an internal dialogue in the mind of the reader. Not only do readers inquire through anticipating questions, but they also justify their thoughts by linking them to facts in the text. Initially, teachers need to make these cues explicit and somewhat exaggerated for emphasis, but eventually the read-think scenario becomes quite fluid. In fact, it becomes embedded in the process of the effective reader.

Active Readers Make Inferences

Best Practice

The read-think strategy fosters inquiry because the reader is forever trying to make inferences and draw conclusions from the text. There are three levels of processing that provide the needed practice for reading between the lines or making good inferences as one reads. These include concrete, representational, and abstract activities. Figure 2 shows how teachers can use these three levels of activities effectively to develop the concept of making inferences and understanding the implied meaning.

Active Readers Visualize

Best Practice

> If the words remain words and sit quietly on the page; if they remain nouns, and verbs and adjectives, then we are truly blind. But, if words seem to disappear and our innermost self begins to laugh and cry, to sing and dance, and finally to fly . . . if we are transformed in all that we are, to a brand new world, then . . . and only then . . . can we READ (Wayman 1981, 1).

The skill of visualization is a skill of literacy, of learning, and of life. To be able to visualize the story in one's mind from the words on the page is what Wayman describes so beautifully. Visualization is critical to the reading process, but it is critical to learning and to life

Making Inferences

Concrete Experience: Reading body language and facial expressions or reading the audience.

Have students role-play various body stances and/or facial expressions: mad, happy, friendly, scared, cold, shy, hot, sad, miserable, joyful . . .

Representational Experience: Reading the implied humor in comics, cartoons and political cartoons

Use three comic strip boxes with a picture in the middle box only. Then have students infer what happened in the first picture and predict what might happen in the last picture.

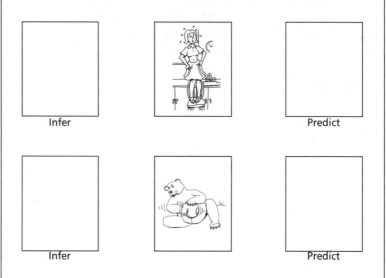

Infer		Predict
Infer		Predict

Abstract Experience: Reading between the lines (going beyond the given information) to draw conclusions (understand the implied meaning of written text).

Have students read a passage and find the implied mood or setting. Use a one-page story or excerpt for them to extrapolate the setting.

Figure 2

as well. The skill of visualization is the skill of goal setting—seeing oneself in a future time and place. It is the skill of achieving excellence—seeing oneself cross the finish line in record time. It is the skill of wellness—seeing oneself healthy and strong.

Use visualization strategies to train students to become better at visualizing. Begin by asking students to think back and re-create images of their bedrooms to determine if the door opens out into the hallway or into the bedroom. Have them recall the refrigerator in their kitchens. Tell them to open the refrigerator door and, in their mind's eye, find the ketchup bottle. Ask them is it full or almost empty? Is it clean or messy?

Then, ask them to think about the times they visualized a new toy or game they wanted. Or when they savored the flavor of a favorite dish Mom cooked. Ask students how often they use the visualization skill.

Next, follow up the memory activity by showing some pictures of optical illusions. Have students sense the shift in perception as they move from one image to the other and try to visualize the two very different pictures. Show them a series of numbers. Hide the numbers and ask them to recall the series by visualizing the sequence.

Finally, connect visualization to reading. Read aloud a scene from a story and ask students to visualize the scene as they re-create the image on paper. Discuss how active readers constantly make pictures in their minds as they read; that is, visualize what they see in their minds' eyes. Suggest that students use this strategy over and over as visualization helps them make meaning of the text.

T Tapping into Prior Knowledge Supports Schema Theory

Schema theory (Pearson 1987) is about comprehending what one reads. Based on the constructivist view of learning, schema theory states that the learner possesses an individually held, personal scheme of things in his or her mind. This scheme is constructed through background knowledge and experiences of the learner. Schema theory suggests that each reader brings a different scheme to the reading, based on background knowledge and life experiences. To read with comprehension, readers must somehow connect the incoming information with the existing scheme in their minds. They must make sense of the input based on what they already know. Thus, if schema theory is true, it is critical to stir up that prior knowledge before learners read to help each reader connect the new to the old. It may be important for teachers to spend more time *before* the reading to create a mind-set for what is going to be read than to spend the time *after* the reading to check on what students comprehended.

Tapping into prior knowledge seems to be the prereading strategy that leads to deep understanding. Knowing that learning is a function of experience, the idea of providing prereading experiences appears to be an essential link to reading comprehension. One way teachers can help students understand is to ask students to agree or disagree with statements about the reading prior to the reading and then again after the reading to compare their ideas. The second way is to ask students to make predictions using the KWL strategy (Ogle 1989) to determine what they know, what they want to know, and what they have learned through the KWL strategy. A third strategy that works well is the BET strategy in which students base on fact, express possibilities, and tender a bet or guess.

These kinds of prelearning strategies promote deep understanding of the reading by putting the emphasis on prior knowledge. The search for meaning is based on the individual scheme of each learner. This meaning-seeking mechanism called the brain fosters connection making and actually creates the neural pathways in the mind of the learner. These pathways are the pathways that enhance memory and learning. In fact, they are necessary for the patterning to occur that chunks the learning for short- and long-term memory (Sylwester 1995).

The Constructivist Approach

Best Practice

Schema theory makes a case for prelearning strategies that tap into prior knowledge. The triangle and the inverted triangle illustrate the traditional and the constructivist way of approaching reading (see Figure 3). Teachers can share these illustrations with students as they discuss why they spend time stirring up ideas prior to reading, rather than merely checking up after the reading.

Instead of spending the majority of the time on recall of ideas to check for comprehension after the reading, teachers need to give more time and attention to bringing up prior knowledge before and during the reading. In this way readers are ready, with the proper mind-set to accept the incoming input. The connection making is facilitated as the reader links prior knowledge to new information.

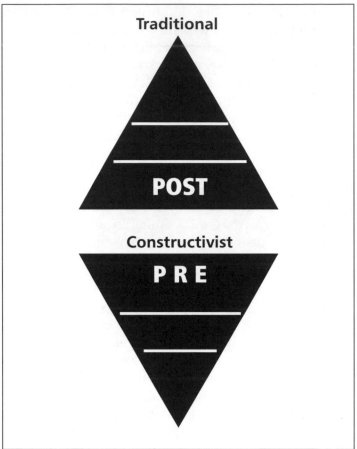

Figure 3

Best Practice ## Use an Agree-Disagree Chart

Another strategy for activating prior knowledge is through the agree-disagree chart. To use this evaluation tool, prepare a listing of statements about the topic for readers to agree or disagree with prior to the reading (see Figure 4 as a sample). Then revisit the statements following the reading to validate answers or allow changes, revisions, and/or additions to initial thinking about the statements.

Agree-Disagree

	BEFORE Agree Disagree	AFTER Agree Disagree
1. Alcohol kills brain cells.		
2. A glass of beer and wine have equal amounts of alcohol.		
3. Marijuana is legal.		
4. Cocaine addiction is chronic, progressive, and fatal.		
5. Prescription drugs are safe.		

Figure 4

SkyLight Professional Development

Best Practice | The KWL Chart

The KWL chart (Ogle 1989) is another prior-knowledge strategy that is powerful to use in K–12 classrooms. Teachers can use a KWL chart (see Figure 5) with students as they discuss the topic or idea they are about to study or read about.

Before reading, have students complete (individually or as a class) the "What we **K**now" and "What we **W**ant to Know" columns. Following the reading, ask students to complete the "What we **L**earned" column. The KWL chart is an efficient way for teachers, as well as students, to find out what students know before the lesson begins.

Best Practice | Prediction

The use of the thinking skill called prediction primes the pump and gets students to tap into prior knowledge and background experiences. The BET strategy works really well to get students to predict. BET stands for the following:

> **B**ase on fact
> **E**xpress possibilities
> **T**ender your bet

Teachers can chunk the reading and have students use the BET cycle. Begin with the title of the piece. Ask students in small groups to look at the facts presented in the title, to think of the possibilities of what the story is about, and then to choose one possibility of what will happen in the story (their bet). Write the bet on large poster paper. Share some of the students' predictions with the whole group. Then have students read in their groups to validate their bets. Students are now

KWL		
What we Know	**What we Want to know**	**What we Learned**

Figure 5

reading with a purpose—to see if they are right or wrong.

Continue through a short piece until students understand the BET strategy. At another time, have them try the same strategy with a nonfiction piece from a textbook. Let them discuss how the BET strategy helps them think and read at the same time.

> *. . . prediction primes the pump and gets students to tap into prior knowledge . . .*

Extensive Reading Encourages Flexible Reading

Good readers read extensively. They read in a variety of settings: silently and mentally to themselves, orally to and with others, and in school with guided reading in groups using particular cueing strategies. Good readers read fiction and nonfiction. They read fiction in many ways through different kinds of literature (called genre) that might include the following: poetry, novels, short stories, folk tales, fairy tales, tall tales, children's stories, adventure stories, mysteries, biographies and autobiographies, science fiction, fantasy, memoirs, and three act plays.

Good readers read all kinds of nonfiction as well. They read articles, essays, critiques and reviews, newspaper editorials and features, and political commentary. They read pamphlets, instruction manuals, brochures, newsletters, memos, and e-mails. Good readers read friendly letters, business letters, greeting cards, posters, and billboards. In short, good readers read. They read everything, everywhere, all the time. In fact, evidence suggests that the gap, sometimes called Mathew Effects (Stanavitch 1986), between good readers and poor readers widens over time as good readers continue to read all the time, and poor readers continue not to read over much time. They seem to never catch up.

When teachers encourage extensive reading in various settings and sample different genre, readers become familiar, fluent, and flexible with the various types of reading material they encounter throughout life. Teachers can sample student-reading preferences by asking students about their preferences, which is a beginning to a lively discussion about comparing and contrasting genre. These types of discussions heighten the awareness of nonreaders as they begin to explore the regions of reading and it propels students who are already voracious readers to investigate new genre.

When teachers encourage extensive reading in various settings and sample different genre, readers become familiar, fluent, and flexible with the various types of reading material . . .

The Human Graph—
An Interactive Experience

Best Practice

Reading, or "reading reading," distinguishes reading time in the classroom that is not for specific skill development but rather for just plain old reading; just for the

enjoyment of reading. This is the time to begin to develop the-kind-of-book-I-like or my-favorite-author atti-
tudes that readers achieve by sampling a range of genres
and authors. To initiate this in the classroom, teachers
might use an interactive experience called the human
graph to begin the conversation about what is appeal-
ing to eager readers and not-so-eager readers.

To try this highly motivating activity, have students
respond to the human graph by going to one side of
the room or the other, basing their preferences on one
of the choices listed after Figure 6 (a human graph example).

Human Graph

| Love Fiction | Like Fiction | Like Both Fiction and Nonfiction | Like Nonfiction | Love Nonfiction |

Figure 6

1. Fiction or Nonfiction
2. Mysteries or Histories
3. Biographies or Autobiographies
4. Tall Tales or Folktales
5. Limericks or Haiku
6. Narrative or Procedural

As the teacher calls out each of the above choices, the students literally move to the designated side of the room. After each move to a category of choice, have students talk with others in their areas about why they made the choices they made. Sample some of their thoughts. You may use the above (1–6) information gathered to design lesson introductions to each genre listed. This practice motivates students to think about the various genre they might want to sample.

The human graph is also useful as students read a story. Just ask them to choose one character or another, one plot line or another, or one setting or another. It is a great way to get them involved in the story once they have found a genre they like.

Use a Venn Diagram to Compare and Contrast

Reading is flexible. Introduce students to various genre, including the following: poetry, textbooks, recipes, instructions, articles, e-mail. Have students use a Venn diagram to compare and contrast two very different kinds of reading material (see Figure 7 as an example). Discuss the genre and the myriad elements of each that creates the richness of a particular reading through the sounds of language, story and plot lines, headlines and graphics, and their relationship to literacy.

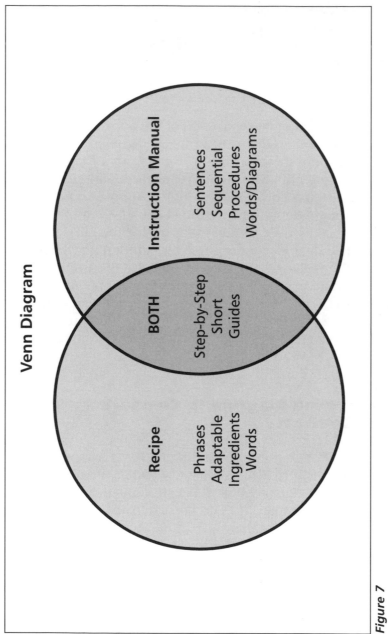

Venn Diagram

Instruction Manual
Sentences
Sequential
Procedures
Words/Diagrams

BOTH
Step-by-Step
Short
Guides

Recipe
Phrases
Adaptable
Ingredients
Words

Figure 7

R Research on the Brain Informs Educational Practice

The emerging research on mind, memory, and learning supports sound pedagogy and also provides new insights about how the brain works. Naturally, this information impacts the literacy community. For example, the concept of constructivism, which holds that the learner constructs meaning in the mind by connecting new information to prior knowledge, is supported by the fact that dendrites, root-like characters that extend from the brain cell to receive messages (Sylwester 1995), continue to grow and interconnect throughout one's lifetime. Further research suggests that dendritic growth can be stimulated by rich environments (Diamond 1998). This logically includes print-rich environments that foster literacy.

The mind typically holds seven bits of information, plus or minus two.

In addition, the concept that memory is stored throughout the brain and can be triggered by any number of sensory stimuli supports the idea of stimulating prior knowledge before reading, as already discussed. The fact that the mind typically holds seven bits of information, plus or minus two, supports a method called chunking of information for ease of memory. Chunking means that certain data are remembered as one collective set, or chunk, for easier recall. It facilitates the memory and learning of discrete bits of information.

Another piece of research links emotion to memory and points once again to the critical role past experience play in the teaching-learning process. To visualize how dendrites develop into an eco-jungle system in the brain, think of the mind as a mind map. Think of themes, such as the ones used in curriculum development, that provide a means to explicit connection making, and think of chunking as a way to facilitate short-term memory by connecting information as one is learning it. HOMES is a meaningful chunk that helps one remember the names of the five Great Lakes:

> **H**uron
> **O**ntario
> **M**ichigan
> **E**rie
> **S**uperior

While these examples just touch the tip of the research iceberg on how the brain learns, they serve to illustrate the powerful linkage between theory and practice.

Sensory Memory to Storage (or Long-Term Memory)

Emerging research on the brain and learning sheds light on the important aspects of the mind, memory, and learning. Using concepts from the research on the brain and learning, think about the following statement and agree or disagree with it:

The brain is more like a sieve than it is like a sponge.

If one agrees with the statement, then one can begin to understand the saying "Memory, the thing I forget with." While it is a bit of a joke, there is the seed of reality in the paradoxical statement. The brain is designed to pay attention to important information and to let go of extraneous information that it does not seem to need. Therefore it does, indeed, act more like a sieve by sifting for the big chunks of information and sifting out the inconsequential.

To understand more fully how the mind-memory-learning system works in the human brain, think about another metaphor, which uses the concept of the computer screen. The memory follows this metaphorical scenario:

It's on my screen (sensory memory).
It's on my desktop (short-term memory).
It's on my menu (working memory).
It's on my hard drive (storage and long-term memory).

It's on My Screen (Sensory Memory)
It's on the screen means some sensory input gets one's attention, which is the first stage of memory. Through novelty, relevance, or meaning, the mind attends to the input. The brain notices the sensory input. For example, a teacher attends a conference and hears that the educational concern is not about technology but rather about the impact of technology. This idea catches the teacher's attention because the teacher is working with computers at school.

It's on My Desktop (Short-Term Memory)
When one makes sense of the input by connecting it to something he or she already knows, the information is in short-term memory, or it is on the computer's

desktop. The teacher in the above example thinks about how technology impacts literacy, and now the information goes into short-term memory. Or, because it is causing dissonance and not connecting properly to something he or she already knows, the teacher is even more aware of the input and it still goes into short-term memory.

It's on My Menu (Working Memory)
Next, one actually uses the new information in some way and it goes on the menu, which represents your working memory. The teacher takes the idea to his or her team and suggests that the team work on the impact of technology and how it changes the reading-writing program plans. Now it is in working memory because the teacher is actually using the information.

It's on My Hard Drive (Storage and Long-Term Memory)
Finally, as the teacher continues to massage the information about the impact of technology, the teacher notices a shift from concern about computers to concern and planning about curriculum impact. It is now on your hard drive and it pops up from long-term memory where it is stored until it is needed.

Have students describe a personal example of how they have remembered something following the metaphor of the computer screen, using as many of the four stages of short- and long-term memory as they can. Share and sample some. Then, talk about how mind-mapping depicts the pathways the mind takes as it connects to various ideas. Have students create a mind map (see Figure 8 as an example) to see how it works and then relate the mind-mapping experience to memory through the concept of neural connection making. Discuss the power of themes, or big ideas, as umbrellas or natural connections that bring thoughts together in the mind of the learner.

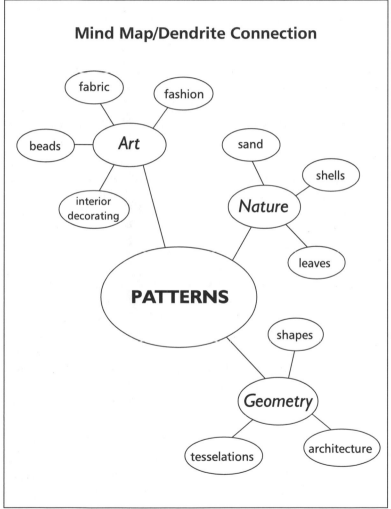

Figure 8

Best Practice **Chunking Information**

Chunking, connecting ideas so that they are recalled as one coherent piece of information, is a memory technique that the mind adapts to easily. There are various chunking methods that help the mind recall bits of information. One way is through the use of mnemonics, a memory device that uses some sound or structure to recall information. HOMES, the mnemonic device for the names of the Great Lakes, was discussed earlier. The rhyme "yours is not to reason why, just invert and multiply" is another mnemonic device used as a way to remember how to divide fractions. Have students think of some mnemonics they have used to recall information and have them share these techniques with others. Talk about how mnemonics help students remember what they read. Demonstrate how mnemonic devices help with recall and, subsequently, with comprehension for better long-term memory and application. Challenge students to create new mnemonic devices.

Another memory device that helps chunk information is the metaphor. The three-legged stool (Waxman and Walberg 1999) is a metaphor for educators to consider in their decision making. There are three elements that interact: the teacher, the student, and the parent. Just like a three-legged stool, all three "legs" are necessary for functionality. Invite students to think of a metaphor that works for them as they try to remember something. Discuss the power of these concrete metaphors in making abstractions more real.

One final thought about chunking concerns the 7+2 principle. The brain remembers seven bits of information, plus or minus two. Think of all the information that falls into that category: Social Security numbers, phone numbers, zip codes, seven deadly sins, seven dwarfs, seven wonders of the world. Encourage students to think of more. Then, whenever possible, explicitly *chunk* information into manageable pieces for easier recall. Assist students with the chunking. Over time they become better at learning a chunk at a time and finally, putting things all together on their own.

A Analysis of Words Promotes Reading Proficiency

"Reading wars" is an ongoing debate in which there have been two camps or two schools of thought in the educational community. Each camp of reading educators endorses an approach to teaching reading. One approach is phonics, in which word-attack skills reign supreme. The other is the whole-language approach, in which literature-based reading takes center stage. However, contrary to the notion of the reading wars—that battle over the ideas of a phonics approach versus a literature-based approach—the reality is that both approaches work together. This "balanced" teaching philosophy is embraced by many reading teachers. While this section highlights the phonics approach, the whole language or literature-based approach is discussed more fully in other sections. However, it is a combination or balance of the phonics and whole-language approaches that is most appropriate for a comprehensive early reading program.

Analysis of words promotes reading competency and proficiency. Skill in decoding unknown words is part and parcel of a good reader's repertoire (Anderson et al. 1984). Complementing a speaking-listening vocabulary that quickly becomes a sight vocabulary for the early reader, word-attack skills are necessary and useful tools to continue building vocabulary. These decoding skills, as they are sometimes called, empower the reader to continue to build a reading-writing vocabulary for fluency.

This decoding umbrella, called word-attack skills, includes the following:

Phonemic awareness: the awareness of sounds

Phonics: the strategy of dissecting the letter sounds and blending them into words

Contextual clues: extracting the meaning of a word from the context in which it is used

Structural analysis: derivatives such as prefixes, suffixes, digraphs, and blends

Phonemic awareness is about building a conscious awareness to the sounds within words. The centerpiece of phonemic awareness is in music, sounds of the city, sounds of the farm, rhyming (cat, hat, sat, bat), and in sounds that are alike (sh-oe, sh-ut, sh-irt), or (f-un, f-amily, f-arm). Phonics is the skill of attaching or matching the proper sound and letter combination (b says ba, t says ta, p says pa).

The mission of the educator is to help young people love to read through the skills of literacy.

When readers are able to enhance their reading-writing-speaking-listening skills in all forms of written and oral communications, their academic achievement blossoms. These are the tools of the literate person. These are the tools that make the difference between loving reading and loathing reading. The mission of the educator is to help young people love to read through the skills of literacy. The skills that create fluent and proficient readers (readers who love to read) include decoding skills.

Direct instruction in word-attack skills is efficient, effective, and appropriate. Surrounding students with the awareness of the sounds around their world is the beginning. Giving them the skills to decode those sounds is the next best step. And enabling them to build their fluency and comprehension through vocabulary is the ultimate goal, for then they are reading efficiently and effectively. Reading becomes a fun activity, not a futile one.

Direct Instruction of Word-Attack Skills

The analysis of words (word-attack skills) include a hierarchy of sorts, beginning with sound awareness and culminating with abilities to derive meaning from root words, prefixes, and suffixes. Also included in the word-attack strategies are contextual clues. Phonemic awareness builds sound awareness; phonics builds sound-letter relationships beginning with a base of hard consonants, soft consonants, and vowels to blends, digraphs, and diphthongs and schwa sounds.

One practical strategy that adapts easily to the early work with decoding skills is the sound book. Teachers can use this strategy to create a sequence of sounds to teach through direct instruction. Hard consonants, blends, vowels, digraphs, and so on are taught, creating a theme for the week. Then, teachers can use that sound to develop meaningful learning experiences that put emphasis and attention on that sound.

For example, if the sound of the week is /p/, various learning experiences are structured to emphasize /p/. Youngsters might pick pumpkins, count the pumpkin seeds, and make pumpkin pie. Each day, students can complete a sound book page which stresses the focus sound through writing and composing. Teachers can send home the sound booklet at the end of the week asking students to read the booklet to anyone and everyone and collect signatures.

A major benefit of keeping a sound booklet is that as students read the booklet over and over they become fluent with the phonics skills. The sound booklet works with younger and older students who need decoding emphasis because the booklet focuses on one sound, providing the needed practice.

Best Practice

Vocabulary Logs

Use vocabulary logs to build vocabulary around the content of disciplines through analysis skills, root words, and derivatives. Have science words, social studies words, and a literature vocabulary to facilitate learning words by themes. Help students become aware and eventually skillful in using the word analysis to figure out unknown words.

Cooperative learning is rated by Joyce (1999a)
as the number one strategy to increase student
achievement and to enhance self-esteem.

C Cooperative Learning Groups Engage Learners

"How do I know what I think until I see what I say" is a paradoxical statement that somehow explains the thinking power of group work. As learners express their thoughts to their team partners, the thinking becomes visible to their peers and to the learners themselves.

The strategy called literature circles (Bjorklund, Handler, Mitten, and Stockwell 1998) taps into powerful learning experiences. Students work in small groups with a selected novel or story. They take on various roles and responsibilities as they read and discuss sections of the book. By putting thoughts from their reading into their own words, learners process the written language in terms that make sense to them. They use their speaking vocabulary to interpret the written language, and in the process, learners clarify and crystallize their own thinking.

Establish Roles and Responsibilities
Best Practice

Through the roles and responsibilities of the group members, all members must participate (Johnson and Johnson 1983; Slavin 1983). One student leads the discussion with predetermined questions. Another shares a favorite passage, while still another might quiz members on selected vocabulary. This team effort builds a sense of trust and safety and a sense of belonging, while at the same time, building a strong understanding of what critical reading is all about. It makes reading active, interactive, and engaging for all members. In fact, cooperative learning is rated by Joyce (1999a) as the number one strategy to increase student achievement and to enhance self-esteem. In over 600 hundred studies cited by the Johnsons (1983) the evidence is clearly positive and convincing.

Cooperative learning makes it easier for students to ask for help in a small, safe setting. It also makes it easier for students to question, share, and critique. When teachers structure cooperative-learning groups as part of the overall reading program, it also inherently opens the door to a multiple intelligences approach to literacy. Using the interpersonal intelligence as one approach, Gardner's (1983) theory suggests seven other entry points to learning: verbal/linguistic (of course), visual/spatial, logical/mathematical, musical/rhythmic, bodily/kinesthetic, intrapersonal, and the naturalist.

Working in teams, learners are able to draw their perception of a particular reading (visual), sequence the events (logical), find the rhythm of the language (musical), dramatize the reading (bodily), keep a reading response journal (intrapersonal) and discern the environmental settings of the readings (naturalist). Imagine the richness of the reading experience in these literature circles. It seems impossible not to be drawn into the web of intrigue as the plot of a story unfolds and as the members of a cooperative learning group enhance that unfolding.

Best Practice — Literature Circles

Cooperative learning strategies that incorporate roles and responsibilities and involve choice within a given structure are highly effective for literacy instruction. Literature circles, based on such strategies, are one way to assist struggling readers.

Similar to book clubs, literature circles (Bjorklund et al. 1998) usually consist of five or six students. If you are trying this practice with your class, note one motivational strategy is to use standard books such as novels rather than picture books. Students often want to read more sophisticated material but need support. While students must read at their developmental level for deep understanding and reading successes, the literature circle gives students the help they need to tackle more advanced books.

To use the literature circles, follow these simple steps:

1. Select themes such as friendship, trust, courage, or fear. Gather four to five books on the theme and let students select a book and form small groups (literature circles) accordingly.

2. Some roles that teachers might assign are:

   Discussion Leader: creates Socratic
        questions for discussion
   Wordsmith: defines significant vocabulary
   Literary Illuminary: illuminates the literary
        sections by reading aloud
   Character Actor: role-plays characters,
        actions, motives, etc.
   Illustrator: Captures key images from the
        reading
   Surveyor: graphs the plot line of the story

   Naturally, the roles played in literature circles should be age-appropriate and suited to students' abilities. For example, very young children might work in threes and have a storyteller, a questioner, and an artist to draw the story as it unfolds.

3. Plot the reading assignments for each book and have students meet to discuss, share, and read aloud, using the assigned roles to keep the group moving along.

4. Use a culminating day for groups to share their books with other groups as students may want to read the other books on their own.

Y You-Are-a-Reader Attitude Matters

Theory

Youngsters from around the world come to school with an unmistakable mission. That mission is to learn to read. They are motivated from within. They want to read. Beyond anything else, youngsters have come to school to learn to read. Preschoolers take those magical picture books, turn the pages ever so deliberately, and mouth words to tell the story they see pictured. They gingerly select those big, fat chapter books and proudly carry them under their arms for all their friends to see. From sixteen months to sixteen years of age, youngsters can enjoy and listen attentively as someone reads aloud from a favorite storybook.

Youngsters know intrinsically that reading matters. It matters a lot. Literacy is the key that unlocks many doors in school and in life. To sustain that sense of wonder and motivation to read is every teacher's mission as well. To keep students coming back for that next book; to develop the skill and the drive for life-long reading; to achieve fluent and flexible reading; to discover reading is informative, instructive, and enjoyable is a major goal of schooling (NAEP 1998).

Constant and continual feedback is a powerful tool.

To fuel that initial thirst for reading that youngsters bring with them to school and to instill a positive you-are-a-reader attitude, constant and continual feedback is a powerful tool (Showers et al. 1998). This feedback sometimes is structured in the form of what Joyce (1999a) calls *feedback loops.* Feedback loops are data-gathering tools that give students and teachers windows into the progress of the learner. For example, a feedback loop might be a graph charting the number of the books read each week or of the new vocabulary words encountered. The feedback loops might be more informal. Students might simply gather word cards or a list of unknown words encountered during one week.

In these formal and informal feedback strategies, teachers encourage students to keep track of their reading, to keep records, and to log data that provide instant, visible, and accessible feedback about their progress. In fact, data are logged for individual students, classes, grade levels, schools, girls, and boys, so that the feedback is comprehensive and yet specific enough to allow mindful decision making. Feedback loops result in a focus that propels the readers involved to read even more.

Teachers can plot the number of books read by the class using a device such as a construction-paper "caterpillar" winding around the highest boundaries of the classroom. Learners respond eagerly to such data on display. As they witness the accumulation of segments in this metaphorical representation of their work, they are inspired to read more and make the caterpillar grow. As the growing caterpillar expands and winds around the room, visual feedback is available to the students. They see every day how the reading is increasing with the class effort. These first data and feedback loops work just as they were intended (Joyce and Wolf 1996). They inspire the competitive spirit and drive students to achieve.

Similarly, the more formalized feedback loops, such as daily, weekly, and monthly data gathering by individual students, classes within the school, and schoolwide surveys, as described by Showers and Joyce (1998), inspire and motivate youngsters on their reading journeys. In turn, the data is available to teachers, parents, and administrators for sound decision making. When the feedback loops note that the fifth-grade boys are low in their daily/weekly numbers, educators can intervene with swift and sure measures.

Best Practice — Data and Feedback Loops

You-are-a-reader attitude means that that students understand that reading matters and they are getting good at it. It is the attitude of the "inner winner" not the "outer doubter." By creating data and feedback loops for good student decision making, students become invested in their own reading progress. They take ownership as they become more advanced with the graphs and charts of their reading progress. These written records empower students to do more as they see the data accumulate and their accomplishments made visible.

To implement the data feedback loops or continuous, pertinent student data, have students keep charts and data logs about the types of books and authors they read. These tools are the feedback loops. As students gather data and represent data, they are able to make better decisions about their learning based on the feedback available. Help them learn to gather data to drive their work and their learning decisions.

Use these ideas to set up data collection sheets for each student to use to gather data:

- Number of books per week
- Types of books (fiction/nonfiction)
- Authors
- Genre
- Other

Summarize data by small group or by the whole class:

- Number of books per week
- Types of books (fiction /nonfiction)
- Authors
- Genre
- Other

Student Portfolios

Best Practice

The student portfolio has been getting a good response from teachers, students, and parents as a feedback tool. A student portfolio is a grand and graphic measure of the growth and development of student learning that inspires the student to do more and to do it even better than last time. While this data is probably considered soft data compared to the hard data of number of books read, the reading portfolio can be an effective tool for self-assessment, goal setting, and evidence of achieving the goals or movement toward the goals. Helping students maintain and sustain their love of reading and attain the goals they have set for themselves is a mission teachers must embrace.

Feedback is the food of champion readers.

Teachers can have their students structure their portfolios around the reading from the literature circles or even around biographies from social studies or science. Students can keep "learning lists" of vocabulary words, authors, genre, reflections on particular readings, and so on. The possibilities are limitless and the feedback is illuminating. After all, feedback is the food of champion readers.

ⓜ Mediate with Early Intervention Strategies

As discussed earlier, the concept that "the rich get richer and the poor get poorer" is the essence of the research findings called Mathew Effects (Stanovitch 1986). Over time, good readers read more and more, and poor readers read less and less or not at all. The gap between them in terms of achievement continues to widen. Stop the madness! Intervene in creative and purposeful ways before the gap widens any more.

Teachers must commit to use what they know about the teaching-learning process to help students conquer reading challenges. Intervention in the literacy instruction process does not mean "Teach it louder and slower." It does not mean "Send them to summer school." It does not mean, "Keep them back." Intervention means doing things differently and, in this case, doing things differently *immediately*. It means using explicit strategies to find the entry point for the learner. Intervention means embracing methods for developing reading fluency and enhancing comprehension.

The burning question: How does one intervene successfully? There are many ways to structure reading interventions, as skillful teachers demonstrate all the time. Two particularly powerful interventions are reciprocal teaching (Palinscar and Brown 1985) and one-to-one tutoring (Bloom 1981) with Roger Farr's model-coach-reflect (MCR) methodology (Farr 2000).

The reciprocal-teaching model delineates four distinct steps that make reading interactive between teacher and students.

These four steps are:

- Summarize
- Question
- Clarify
- Predict

The teacher models and a designated student-leader practices reciprocally. More specifically, the teacher summarizes the reading, poses questions that come to mind, clarifies concerns, and predicts what may happen next in the reading. The process models explicitly what good readers do mentally as they read. As each student takes responsibility for leading the reading discussion, he or she follows the four-step cycle of summarizing, questioning, clarifying, and predicting about a passage from the reading.

Another effective intervention is one-to-one tutoring (Bloom 1981). To enhance this intervention, teachers can couple it with three procedures outlined by Roger Farr (1999): modeling, coaching, and reflection (MCR). In a one-on-one situation, teachers can explicitly model their behavior while reading aloud, demonstrating the interactive nature of the text and the thinking of the reader. Then teachers can enter into *coached practices* with individual learners. During coached practices, teachers provide specific, immediate feedback, which stimulates students to think reflectively. In these coached practices, teachers ask students to say out loud what they are thinking as they read and to give reasons for that thinking.

Coaching in the reading instruction process is a strategy to make the implicit reactions to the reading more explicit. In this way, students can further examine their thought processes as they continue to read. They can examine and reflect on what is occurring in the text and in their minds and they can anticipate what is about to happen. Teachers mediate this stage for metacognitive reflection with questions that call for student self-monitoring. They ask what connections the student is making, how they might relate the ideas to a personal situation, or, simply, what they think will happen next and why. Often, teachers implement reciprocal teaching with small groups, but when the teacher is able to work with one student the teacher can choose strategies that are in direct relation to the student's miscues. This creates a diagnosis-prescription cycle tailored to the explicit deficiencies of the learner. It is mediation (Feuerstein et al. 1980) by the teacher that is direct, intentional, and meaningful. According to Bloom, there is no teaching as effective as the one-to-one tutorial.

Best Practice ## Reciprocal Teaching

Swift and appropriate interventions are necessary when students are having difficulty with reading. A system of diagnosis and prescription is standard practice; intervention means to note deficiencies in literacy and to address them with appropriate strategies. Intervention is based on the Mathew Effects research in which Stanovitch (1986) suggests that the reading gap continues to widen as students progress through school. In other words, even though reading is becoming more prevalent in curriculum, readers read more and more while nonreaders read less and less or not at all. In essence, the rich (readers) get richer and the poor (nonreaders) get poorer.

In this well-researched reading strategy called reciprocal teaching (Palinscar and Brown 1985), a four step procedure (summarize, question, clarify, and predict) makes the reading process interactive between the teacher and the text. Initially, the teacher works with small groups of students to model the reciprocal teaching procedures. The teacher reads a paragraph or two and then summarizes what he or she just read. Then, the teacher poses questions for discussion and deliberation. The teacher models how to clarify the meaning of the text and then asks students to make predictions about what might happen next and why.

For example, a teacher asks students to summarize in their own words the information they have just read about the formation of volcanoes. Then, the teacher asks students to generate questions that come to mind as they learn how volcanoes are formed. Once students produce some questions, the teacher makes clarifications and asks students to predict what might occur next in the reading based on their thinking at the moment. As students read to validate the predictions, in essence, they read more intently because the reading has a clear and compelling purpose.

In the reciprocal teaching model, after the teacher models the procedure a number of times and explains the process as he or she is modeling it, it is time for students to reciprocate. A designated student-leader models the same process the teacher has been demonstrating. The student assumes the role of teacher and repeats the process.

For example, a student reads a brief portion of text about the explorers in the New World. The student-leader encourages the student to summarize in his or her own words what he or she has just read. The student-leader proceeds to ask questions about the explorers' adventures. As the student-leader clarifies understandings about the reading, he or she elicits predictions by asking, for instance: What do you think the explorers are thinking? feeling? How might you feel in a similar situation? What are their options? What might you do if you were part of this team? In this way, each student, in turn and over time, becomes the student-leader and models the read-think strategy of reciprocal teaching.

One by one, students take over responsibility for the active, attentive read-think process of critical readers. The leadership role is reciprocal, turning over responsibility to the students, and in reciprocating, students eventually internalize the reading process. Reciprocal teaching is a reading strategy that works well as an intervention because it provides a model of reading for students to practice explicitly. It is structured for success as students take on the role of the leader and learn to use the strategies on their own.

One-to-One Tutoring

Best Practice

Another method of intervention is one-to-one tutoring, using the modeling-coaching-reflection (MCR) strategy (Farr 2000). Teachers can use this strategy before, during, and after reading to help students see how readers comprehend what they are reading.

Before reading, the teacher models the talk-aloud strategy to demonstrate what he or she is thinking about the title of the story. As the teacher thinks aloud about the title, he or she makes predictions about what the reading will be about and gives reasons for those predictions.

At various points during the reading, the teacher stops and thinks aloud and he or she predicts what will happen next. The teacher talks aloud to explain why he or she is thinking that might happen. The teacher uses inferences for implied meaning and talks about how the words suggest certain things.

After the reading, the teacher summarizes his or her interpretation of the text and justifies it with specific examples in the text. The emphasis here is on comprehending what one is reading while one is reading—not on comprehending the reading after the reading. The teacher uses this process—the modeling-coaching-reflection strategy—with that emphasis in mind.

In a one-to-one scenario, the student practices the talk-aloud strategy with appropriate coaching by the teacher. The teacher asks, "Why are you thinking that? What makes you so sure? Where is the evidence in the text?" This coaching leads to a reflective summary by the student of how he or she responded to the reading. The MCR model eventually becomes second nature to students as they learn to read and think while reading.

It takes the combined efforts of the teacher, the student, and the parent/guardian to support the academic schooling of the youngster.

Appealing to Parents/ Guardians Gets Them Involved

 Waxman and Walberg (1999) describe schooling as a three-legged stool. They explain that the first leg of the stool is the teacher, the second leg is the student, and the third leg is the parent/guardian. Without all three legs, the stool is not functional. It takes the combined effort of the three legs to support the stool properly. In other words, it takes the combined efforts of the teacher, the student, and the parent/guardian to support the academic schooling of the youngster.

Waxman and Walberg's metaphor embraces research that suggests that parent/guardian involvement in students' school experience is vital. When parents/guardians get involved, student benefits are great. This involvement may mean that parents/guardians volunteer time in the classroom, that they become active in parent groups at the school, or that they simply support the academic efforts of their children at home.

Of course, the most common involvement at home is parents/guardians helping their children with their homework or at least monitoring the homework situation and seeing that it does get done. By being aware of the assignments and supervising the process, parents/guardians are implicitly supporting their children's academic progress in school. They have some sense of the content students are learning and they have some connection to the schoolwork.

Another way parents/guardians support the learning of their children, especially in the early grades, is by reading aloud to their children at home or reading along with older children. As one principal tells her parents, "You don't have to read with your child every day, just the days that you eat" (Anonymous respondent at Teaching for Intelligence Conference Literacy Q/A Panel, March 2000, Orlando, FL). She makes her point with humor, but she makes her point. Reading with children is as critical to their growth as food is.

This support effort involves creating a home environment that is rich in print materials: magazines, books, booklets, newspapers, and journals. It is also important for students to have library cards and to take frequent trips to borrow books. Students also benefit from seeing their parents/guardians reading and discussing what they have read. Students see that reading is a lifelong endeavor and they begin to emulate the parent/guardian behaviors in literacy.

Parents/guardians . . . often want to participate in their children's school experience; sometimes they just need some cues . . .

Getting parents, guardians, the extended family, and even the community at large involved must be a strategic, deliberate, and collaborative goal of classroom teachers and school leaders. Of course, the most common way to do this is through frequent communications and invitations to participate in school activities. Parents/guardians often want to participate in their children's school experience; sometimes they just need some cues about how to do that.

Homework
Best Practice

Homework is an integral part of the teaching-learning process. It is the time for students to try things on their own—some independent practice. However, involved parents/guardians provide valuable support. They make homework part of the daily routines at home. Simply by scheduling time for homework and providing a place for the student to do the work, parents/guardians send a clear and important message to their children: homework is important.

Of course, sometimes students need hands-on help to understand the homework, and many parents willingly get involved at this level when they can or when they understand the process the teacher has outlined. Older siblings can provide some guidance here, too. The important factor is the availability and accessibility of the parent/guardian, family, or extended family in the homework process to provide the necessary support for the student to succeed.

Best practice suggests that educators instruct parents/guardians in how they might best help their children with homework. Teachers can easily delineate the roles parents/guardians play in getting involved in homework matters. For example, parents/guardians can structure a time and a place for homework that becomes a part of their child's routine. Parents/guardians can be available if their child is stuck on an assignment, having their child explain the homework for further clarity and understanding. All of these parent/guardian behaviors send a clear message to the child that the parent/guardian and teacher are partners in schooling. This kind of parent/guardian participation sets a tone of cooperation and collaboration between the school and home.

Read Aloud

Best Practice

Reading is not just a school activity. Reading is a life skill. Parents/guardians who read at home model the lifelong behavior of reading as a part of everyday life. Parents/guardians who read to their children are giving them the greatest gift of all. They are giving their children the legacy of reading. Early readers are often those children who have experienced frequent reading at home from the time they were infants. They understand that reading is related to the written word and they quickly become adept at figuring out letter-sound relationships and acquiring a sight vocabulary.

Teachers can encourage parents/guardians to read to their children in early grades in a number of ways. Teachers can talk to parents/guardians at parent night, send memos home, create a list of instructions to guide the reading aloud at home, or even establish a tracking activity or incentive program to motivate reading at home.

T Teach Vocabulary with Key Words

The act of reading calls for several critical elements to interact simultaneously: word knowledge, fluency, comprehension, and writing (Shanahan 1998, Cunningham 1994). Students need to develop an extensive vocabulary to read with fluency. In turn, fluency in reading leads to increased comprehension. Fluency also comes from the written language of the reader since the student writes words he or she knows. Increased comprehension enhances the written language of the learner.

Students read what they write with fluency and comprehension because it is their story written in their own words—words they know and comprehend. These words comprise the *key vocabulary,* or the inner language, of learners. These are their "first words" and the "next words" are the more formal vocabulary they add to this organic, natural language of their speaking vocabulary.

The concept of first words-next words focuses on the element of word knowledge as it relates to reading. First words-next words is a method of vocabulary development for a sight vocabulary that enhances vocabulary development through phonemic awareness, phonics, and structural analyses. Sight words are at the heart of the case for word knowledge as it relates to fluency.

Speaking-listening vocabulary and reading-writing vocabulary are inextricably linked . . .

It is important to note that vocabulary development encompasses a speaking-listening vocabulary, as well as a reading-writing vocabulary. While the speaking-listening vocabulary is initially more expansive than the reading-writing vocabulary, the combinations are inextricably linked in the mind of the learner. In fact, the speaking-listening vocabulary often provides the cues for the rhythm and sound of the language that translate into the reading-writing vocabulary. And, at the same time, the reading-writing vocabulary can enrich and enhance the speaking-listening vocabulary through a richness of topics that the reader may encounter or write spontaneously.

Teachers can strengthen this link in powerful ways with organic reading-writing programs (Ashton-Warner 1972) that tap into the natural language of the learner. In this type of program, the inner language of the learner is used to provide a personal vocabulary. The student uses these first words to build written stories that encourage fluent reading. Sylvia Ashton-Warner devised this method of teaching reading to Maori children in New Zealand to facilitate learning for 5–12-year-olds who spoke only their native language. In trying to teach the children to read English, she began with the *organic* vocabulary, which she called the key vocabulary, or words in their native tongue—words from their inner selves. She wrote stories with this vocabulary for the children to read and the children wrote their own stories to read. Gradually, she transitioned the children into proper English.

In essence, organic reading-writing programs suggest ways for students to write words from their speaking-listening vocabulary and to use organic word collections to spark the reading-writing process. Students can manipulate a personally relevant listing of words into written pieces that they can read with fluency and understanding. Students can collect their words over time on word cards, which they can place in word boxes (Showers et al. 1998) or in vocabulary logs or journals. Students manage the boxes, logs, or journals as the *owner* of the words and update them on a regular basis. Students routinely keep the individual lists current, which encourages meaningful use in reading-writing activities. Accompanied with a more structured and formal reading program, the development of an organic vocabulary for the reading-writing–speaking-listening processes facilitate the overall literacy skills of the learner.

Word Boxes

Best Practice

Building a fluent vocabulary through the use of personal word boxes is an easy strategy to use across the disciplines. This is how readers use their natural language and speaking vocabulary to develop a personal reading vocabulary or key vocabulary as Sylvia Ashton-Warner called it. It is also an effective method for students to build vocabulary in core content areas.

To create personal word boxes in the early grades, shoeboxes can be decorated for individual word boxes. To help students gather new words each day, the teacher keeps a supply of 8-inch by 3-inch colored construction paper strips in a coffee can. As students go to the teacher to select their special or key word for the day, they ask the teacher to print the word on the strip. They then trace it, say it, and use it in context before leaving the teacher.

As students collect words on word cards they use the words in their own boxes to play "Go Fish" with a partner. They usually play the card game as soon as they come into the room. They dump the cards from both boxes on the floor and then "Go Fish" for their word cards. Students mix their cards with a partner. Then each student takes a turn picking up a word that is facedown and tries to say the word. If the student knows the word, he or she keeps it and puts it in the word box. If the student does not know the word, he or she puts it back in the pile. If there are any leftover words that no one claims, they are simply thrown away. That way, the owner of the box knows all words in the box and can use them easily in writing and other work.

After students play "Go Fish" with their old words, they are ready for a new word. They then go to the teacher for the word they want for that day. Students may have any word they want. They usually select a word that means something to them. The word is part of some experience or instance in their lives.

The teacher may then have students study their words by using paints, sand, shells, clay, water, blocks, computers, pantomine and/or song to create the letters and spell the words. Once students study their new words, have students put their word strips together to create a story. Stories can be a few words, a phrase, or a sentence or two. Provide function words (the, and, is, this) as needed on neutral color strips.

Make sure students write their sentences each day. In the beginning the "sentence" may only consist of one word, usually a noun. As students add verbs, the sentences eventually grow in length and complexity. Encourage students to add a cover and pictures to illustrate their stories. Change the word strip color each month so the covers of the storybooks and word strips are the same color. In this way, students create storybooks each month with a colorful cover that matches the words in the word boxes for the month. Much like student portfolios, these storybooks show the developmental progress of the learner. September's booklets and stories look different when compared to January's as January's storybooks look different when compared to June's.

Send the storybooks featuring these "organic word stories" home, and ask students to read their books to everyone and then gather signatures for a weekly classroom contest. Encourage students to read their storybooks to Mom, Dad, other family members, friends, or neighbors. Each time students read their booklets, have them gather signatures from "witnesses." The goal is to get them to read the books many times and to read with fluency and comprehension. In essence, students learn to read fluently as this speaking vocabulary becomes their reading and writing vocabulary.

Best Practice   ## Journals and Logs

To develop vocabulary for the older students, word logs or vocabulary journals serve the same purpose as the word boxes. Again, students can use these growing lists of words in their writing or to better understand content-specific reading material. Vocabulary journals or logs work on the same principle as the word boxes, but are geared for the older, more mature students.

Technology Impacts Literacy

Technology impacts reading. As anyone who has a computer nearby knows, the compulsion to go to the computer is always there. It beckons one to write, to compute, to create graphics, to preview films, to purchase online books, to download news articles, to e-mail a friend, to surf the World Wide Web, or just to check the weather. It calls one to use all the skills of literacy: reading, writing, speaking, and listening. Once one answers the call, it is very hard to shut that computer down and move on to other tasks. The computer has a compelling quality not unlike a magnet. Once one logs onto the computer, the pull to stay is great—no matter what the age of the user.

The computer just might be the motivation students need to get hooked on literacy.

With this inherent attraction to technology, do not overlook the power of this enticing tool. The computer just might be the motivation students need to get hooked on literacy (Technology Counts 1998; November, 2000). When students work in pairs or small groups to peer coach and support each other as they explore technological innovations, their engagement in literacy becomes seamless. Think about the possibility for the "i-generation"—the information generation. Literacy online is what it is all about. Literacy online is the format for the new millennium: word processing for letters, stories, and essays; e-mail to communicate with classmates, friends, parents/guardians, and pen pals around the world; spreadsheets to organize and analyze data and feedback; graphic design programs for school and/or class presentations; and the Internet for research. The possibilities are endless as students in today's schools gain more access to computers and as the power of technology becomes fully realized as a champion for the literacy challenge.

Best Practice ## Literacy Online

Literacy online is a way to make technology a part of literacy and learning. Technology is an entry point for motivating literacy skills. Students can use the computer for word processing, e-mail, spreadsheets, graphical presentations, and research to stimulate the reading-writing process. Teachers can use peer editors and partner work and teach Internet formats (formatting for e-mail, chat rooms, what and when to download, what and when to just read on-line, and so on). Literacy online has its own form and function protocols that teachers need to include in the curriculum. Use the following formats purposefully and frequently in classroom activities:

Word Processing
- Writing, editing (cut-and-paste, "spell-check," and bold/italics), rewriting, formatting, keyboarding
- Comparing and contrasting rambling text that has poor spelling and grammar errors to clear, concise, orderly text written with purpose and direction

E-mail
- Communicating with other classrooms, schools, parents/guardians, pen pals
- Contacting experts in a particular field under study

Spreadsheets
- Collecting, organizing, and manipulating data
- Developing budgets or other numerical data

Graphic arts
- Adding graphics, slides, and sound to presentations, speeches, book reports, or even show-and-tell
- Creating illustrations and art for stories, poems, dramas, or essays

Research
- Searching the Internet to research a topic and to learn how to search, survey, prioritize, and to evaluate critically
- Using information efficiently and intelligently for purposeful learning

E Entry Points Honor Multiple Intelligences

Howard Gardner's (1983) work in the area of multiple intelligences has produced a theory that is embraced fully by the educational community. Basically, the theory states that the human mind has multiple intelligences, as opposed to the notion of general intelligence traditionally held.

Using a number of criteria, Gardner has identified eight intelligences to date: verbal/linguistic, visual/spatial, mathematical/logical, musical/rhythmic, bodily/kinesthetic, interpersonal/social, intrapersonal/reflective, and the naturalist/physical world.

Gardner postulates a possible ninth or as he has called it, the eight-and-one-half intelligence—the existential or cosmic intelligence. He is looking to neurologists for information on a processing locale in the brain for the big questions about life and the universe—the philosophical questions that are pondered by poets and priests and people of all ages and in all stages of life.

Gardner defines an intelligence as a way of creating products or solving problems that are valued in at least one culture. He suggests that there are many ways of knowing and of expressing what one knows about the world and that schooling might use all entry points for learners. These entry points tap into the strengths of the individual learners and allow them entry into the learning. The skillful teacher uses a repertoire of strategies based on the eight intelligences.

The intelligences are defined briefly below with some examples to illustrate their various manifestations in K–12 classrooms.

Verbal/Linguistic
Reading, writing, speaking, listening (e.g., drama, stories, narratives, expository writing, speeches, debates, dialogues)

Visual/Spatial
Art, graphics, architecture, sculpture, mapping, navigation (e.g., perspectives, images, advertising, billboards, the imaginary world)

Mathematical/Logical
Mathematics, science, logic, deductive thinking, inductive reasoning (e.g., geometry, algebra, calculus, formulas and equations)

Musical/Rhythmic
Music, rhythm and beat (e.g., composing, singing, playing an instrument, band, orchestra, quartets, symphonies, harmonies)

Bodily/Kinesthetic
Hands-on, manipulatives (e.g., lab work, field trips and experiential learning, role-plays, drama, acting)

Interpersonal/Social
Cooperating, collaborating (e.g., teamwork, leadership, communicating, resolving conflicts, mediating, building relationships)

Intrapersonal/Reflective
Inner self, metacognition (e.g., self-awareness, self-regulatory, self-monitoring, self-assessing, awareness of strengths and weaknesses)

Naturalist/Physical World
Nature and environmental understandings, classifications (e.g, awareness of flora and fauna, classification of species, nature walks and expeditions)

The theory of multiple intelligences provides a viable framework for academic understandings. As teachers tap these various intelligences, they provide students with numerous entry points into literacy and learning. Students can *read* music; they can *read* faces; they can *read* charts, graphs, and illustrations; and they can *read* words. Students can read directions, instructions, factual data, and fine literature. As a result, when students face a complex task, they can engage several intelligences to unravel the intricate layers of thinking and performing to complete the task.

Best Practice — Multiple Intelligences Profile

To develop awareness of the multiple intelligences, organize eight different activities that cause students to use the various intelligences specifically. For example, a teacher may use some optical illusions for students to measure their abilities in the visual/spatial intelligence. As students complete the activities, have them create a personal bar graph of their own personal profiles. Before students begin the activities, have them fold an 8-inch by 11-inch piece of paper into eight vertical folds—similar to a paper fan. Have them label each bar (created by the folds) as an intelligence. The chart serves as a bar graph of sorts, as students mark each bar low, medium, or high based on their personal evaluation of each of their intelligences.

As the graph builds, encourage students to share their profiles with others. Typically they begin to see why it is beneficial to have very different profiles on a team because they complement each other. In this way, students can celebrate the diversity in a team and become aware of the strengths and weaknesses in the various intelligences, especially in the verbal/linguistic, the logical/mathematical and the visual/spatial areas, which impact most directly on the literacy skills.

Best Practice — Multiple Intelligences Grid

To have students become involved in developing literacy activities for each of the eight intelligences, use the planning tool called the MI Grid (see Figure 9).

Multiple Intelligences Grid

VERBAL/LINGUISTIC	LOGICAL/ MATHEMATICAL	VISUAL/SPATIAL	BODILY/ KINESTHETIC

MUSICAL/ RHYTHMIC	INTERPERSONAL/ SOCIAL	INTRAPERSONAL/ REFLECTIVE	NATURALIST/ PHYSICAL

Figure 9

SkyLight Professional Development

Using the headings for the eight intelligences (visual, verbal, musical, mathematical, bodily, interpersonal, intrapersonal, naturalist), have a team of students work together to brainstorm lists of literacy activities and learning experiences for each of the eight intelligences. Then, using the MI Grid of activities to tap into all the intelligences, have students select from the various activities as they take ownership for their own learning. Teachers may want to require one activity choice for each of the intelligences to give some balance to the types of activities students do.

R Read-Aloud, Read-Along, Read-Appropriately Practices Foster Flexible Readers

Based on the National Assessment of Educational Progress (NAEP 1998) framework, there are three types of reading that dictate student proficiency: narratives (for literary experiences), informational reading (for facts, data, and a knowledge base), and procedural reading (for following directions and understanding technical works).

Further suggested in this model are four levels of reading: initial understanding, interpretation, developing a personal response, and evaluating. To help students become efficient and flexible readers moving through the different levels of proficiency, the three strategies of read-aloud, read-along, and read-appropriately play different roles.

Reading aloud gives students the opportunity to hear the sound and rhythm of the language. As the teacher thinks aloud about what he or she is reading, the students begin to understand the connections between the words on the page and what they mean. When students read orally, they, too, can hear the words as they process them.

In the read-along strategy, teachers provide needed word prompts and cues, as well as fluency in the reading act. As students follow along, their pacing is propelled by the fluency of the reader. The read-along is a reading exercise for the classroom and for the home. Parents/guardians and older siblings can read orally as the student reads along.

Surprisingly, the fluent reader can read along at quite a brisk pace and the student somehow seems to keep up, carried along by the flow of the oral reading. (When read-alongs are employed as a strategy for fluency, do not point to the words, but rather place a paper marker beneath the line being read).

Read-appropriately promotes the policy of reading material at an appropriate instructional level for greatest individual gains. The adage "different strokes for different folks" applies well here. As readers respond differently to the reading-writing process, their skill level is critical to their developmental progress. Read-aloud, read-along, and read-appropriately are a triad of strategies that effectively achieve the results teachers want.

National Assessment Educational Progress (NAEP) Matrix Framework

Discuss the NAEP framework for types of reading and levels of comprehension to inform students of the various types of reading. In this way, teachers expose them to the idea of flexible reading for different purposes. Included in the types of reading are narrative for literary experiences, informative for information gathering, and procedural for following directions. Demonstrate each type. Then discuss or think about the levels of reading comprehension: initial understanding, interpretation, personal response, evaluation. Develop a rubric with students that helps them begin to assess their own levels of understanding about their reading (see Figure 10). Discuss the differences and make them aware of the ultimate goal of deep understanding of the reading.

Use Read-Aloud, Read-Along, and Read-Appropriately Strategies

Read-aloud, read-along, and read-appropriately strategies involve three phases of reading instruction. Read aloud using a story, a quote, or short children's book about literacy to model the skills of reading. Some juvenile literature books that highlight the idea of being literate are the following: *Leo the Late Bloomer* by Robert Kraus, *Thank You, Mr. Falker* by Patricia Polacco, and *The Jolly Postman* by Janet and Allan Ahlberg.

To support read-along and read-appropriately, use a four-corner framework to delineate the classroom climate, the skills needed, interaction patterns, and metacogntive reflection. Use the four-corner framework to tie literacy to the microcosm of the classroom (see Figure 11).

For climate, create a safe emotional climate for learning to read. Foster a safe environment in which students have choices about their reading. Also, make sure that students have challenging books to read

Rubric

	INITIAL	INTERPRETIVE	PERSONAL	EVALUATIVE
NARRATIVE	Retells	Makes sense of text	Relates to	Critiques
INFORMATIVE	Summa-rizes	Makes connections	Uses analogy	Reads critically
PROCEDURAL	Repeats	Rephrases	Adapts	Edits essence

Figure 10

Setting the Climate *for* Thinking	Teaching the Skills *of* Thinking
Emotions Choice Challenge Print Rich	Phonemic Awareness Phonics Configural Clues Contextual Clues
Structuring the Interaction *with* Thinking	Thinking *about* Thinking
Literature Circles Peer Editing Readers' Theater Preferences	Reflections Reading Response Journals Data and Feedback Read Aloud

Figure 11

SkyLight Professional Development

within a print-rich environment that offers rigor and robustness in reading materials.

For the skills section, provide direct instruction of reading skills including phonemic awareness to emphasize sounds; phonics for sound word relationships; and configural, contextual, and structural clues to enhance vocabulary and fluency.

For interaction, consider meaningful learning experiences including literature circles (Bjorklund et al. 1998), in which small groups share the reading and discussion of a story or novel, though peer mediation or editing, readers' theater, drama, and read-aloud opportunities.

Finally, for metacognition, or thinking about thinking, provide opportunities for written and oral reflections, reading response journals in which students respond to the reading by writing a journal entry, data/feedback loops, and opportunities for students to think about their reading preferences.

Strategic Reading Is Guided Reading

"Reading is reading is reading" is not the whole story. Reading takes on many forms. Reading is glancing through a piece, skimming and scanning for key thoughts or idea. Reading is singing the lyrics from a page of music to the melodic accompaniment of a piano. Reading is reading an essay for needed edits, revisions, and rewrites. Reading is done in many ways for many reasons.

As the purpose for reading changes, the way one reads changes with it. Look at two very different kinds of reading: reading a short story or reading a textbook. Reading a short story is invitational, as the plot line heightens and the reader anticipates what will happen next. The purpose of reading a short story is often merely for entertainment.

Reading a textbook is quite different. It is reading for information to gain an understanding and a knowledge base about the topic at hand. For some, it is a tedious kind of reading, requiring an especially attentive mind to absorb the essential information.

In both these cases, one can apply different strategies to guide the reading. In fact, two popular guided-reading strategies that are effective and direct interventions are directed-reading-thinking activity (DRTA) (Stauffer1969) and the survey-question-read-recite-review (SQ3R) method (Robinson 1970).

The DRTA strategy lends itself to the short story or other fictional pieces as it directs the reader to use the think-ahead–read–think-back strategy as he or she proceeds through the piece. On the other hand, the SQ3R is perfectly tailored for textbook reading. *Survey* the chapter for boldface type, graphics, and questions at the end; form key *questions* to answer while reading; *read*; *recite* answers; and *review* as needed.

Directed-Reading-Thinking Activity (DRTA)

To use the strategic reading strategy called the DRTA, select a fictional piece for reading and chart out appropriate sections of the story by drawing a line beneath the section to separate the various parts. Have students make predictions about the story by telling partners what they think will happen in that section. Be sure to have them justify their predictions. Then have them read to validate their predictions. Get them to infer, or read between the lines, about a character's feelings and the mood of the story or setting by trying to go beyond the given information. Continue directing the reading by sections with predictions, justifications, inferences, and validations. Direct the reading and the thinking activity and see what happens with students' reading comprehension.

Survey-Question-Read-Recite-Review (SQ3R)

To use the SQ3R strategy for reading a nonfiction piece, walk through SQ3R method with the students using a chapter from a textbook.

> Survey the chapter (headings, subheadings, illustrations, charts, graphics, questions within and at the end of the chapter)
>
> Question (i.e., formulate questions to answer as a check on the main ideas and important information in the chapter)
>
> Read by sections
>
> Recite in your own words what you just read
>
> Review to validate your thinking

Once students have tried the SQ3R method as a guided activity, discuss their reactions to it and the pros and cons. Then have them try the same process in small groups, assigning roles and responsibilities for the questioning, reading, reciting, and reviewing.

Encourage students to use the SQ3R strategy on their own and give some feedback on it.

Bibliography

Allington, R. 1983. The reading instruction provided readers of differing abilities. *Elementary School Journal* 83: 548–559.

Anderson, R., C. Hiebert, J. A. Scott, and I. Wilkinson. 1985. *Becoming a nation of readers.* Champaign: University of Illinois, Center for the Study of Reading.

Ashton-Warner, S. 1972. *Teacher.* New York: Vinton.

Berliner, D., and U. Casanova. 1993. *Putting research to work.* Arlington Heights, IL: Skylight Training and Publishing.

Bjorklund, B., N. Handler, J. Mitten, and G. Stockwell. 1998. *Literature circles: A tool for developing students as critical readers, writers, and thinkers.* Paper presented at the 47th annual conference of the Connecticut Reading Association, Waterbury, CT.

Bloom, B. 1981. *All our children learning: A primer for parents, teachers, and educators.* New York: McGraw-Hill.

Burns, B. 1999. *The mindful school: How to teach balanced reading and writing.* Arlington Heights, IL: Skylight Training and Publishing.

Cawalti, G. 1995. *Handbook of research on improving student achievement.* Arlington, VA: Educational Research Service.

Chall, J. 1983. *Learning to read: The great debate.* New York: McGraw-Hill.

Cunningham, P., and D. Hall. 1994. *Making words: Multi-level, hands-on developmentally appropriate spelling and phonics activities.* Torrence, CA: Good Apple.

———. Undated. *Practical phonics activities that build skills and teach strategies.* Torrence, CA: Staff Development Resources.

Diamond, M., and J. Hopson. 1998. *Magic trees of the mind: How to nurture your child's intelligence, creativity and healthy emotions from birth through adolescence.* New York: Dutton.

English, E. W. 1999. *Gift of literacy for the multiple intelligences classroom.* Arlington Heights, IL: SkyLight Training and Publishing.

Feuerstein, R., Y. Rand, M. B. Hoffman, and R. Miller. 1980. *Instrumental enrichment.* Baltimore: University Park Press.

Flavell, J. 1979. Metacognitions and cognitive monitoring: A new area of child development inquiry. *Applied Psychology* 34: 906–911.

Fogarty, R. 1994. *The mindful school: How to teach for metacognitive reflection.* Arlington Heights, IL: IRI/Skylight Training and Publishing.

Fogarty, R. 2001. *Ten things new teachers need to succeed.* Arlington Heights, IL: SkyLight Training and Publishing.

Gardner, H. 1983. *Frames of mind: The theory of multiple intelligences.* New York: Basic Books.

Johnson, D., R. Johnson, and E. Johnson Holebec. 1983. *Circles of learning: Cooperation in the classroom.* Alexandria, VA: ASCD.

Joyce, B. R. 1999. The great literacy problem and success for all. *Phi Delta Kappan* 81(2): 129–133.

Joyce, B. R. 1999. Reading about reading. *The Reading Teacher,* April, 662–671.

Joyce, B. R., and J. Wolf. 1996. Readersville: Building a culture of readers and writers. In *Learning experiences in school renewal,* edited by Bruce Joyce and Emily Calhoun, 95–96. Eugene, OR: ERIC Clearinghouse.

Kesselman-Turkle, J., and F. Peterson. 1981. *Test-taking strategies.* Chicago: Contempory Books.

Keene, E. O., and S. Zimmerman. 1997. *Mosaic of thought: Teaching comprehension in a reader's workshop.* Portsmouth, NH: Heinemann.

Miller, L. L. 1980. *Developing reading efficiency.* Minneapolis, Minnesota: Burgess Publishing Company.

National Assessment of Educational Progress (NAEP). 1998. Long term trends in student reading performance. *NAEP Facts* 3(1).

Ogle, D. 1989. Implementing strategic teaching. *Educational Leadership* 46(4): 47–48, 57–60.

Palinscar, A.S., and A.L. Brown. 1985. Reciprocal teaching: Activities to promote reading with your mind. In *Reading, thinking and concept development: Strategies for the classroom,* edited by T.L. Harris and E.J. Cogen. New York: College Board.

Palocco, P. 1998. *Thank you, Mr. Falker.* New York: Philomel Books.

Pearson, P. D. 1987. Twenty years of research in comprehension. In *The context of school based literacy,* edited by T. Raphael. New York: Random House.

Robinson, F. P. 1970. *Effective study.* New York: Harper &Row.

Rothstein, E., and G. Lauber. 2000. *Writing as learning: A content-based approach.* Arlington Heights, IL: SkyLight Training and Publishing.

Shanahan, T. 1998. Twelve studies that have influenced K–12 reading instruction. *Illinois Reading Council Journal* 26(1): 50–58.

Showers, B., B. Joyce, M. Scalon, and C. Schnaubelt. 1998. A second chance to learn to read. *Eduacational Leadership,* March, 27–31.

Slavin, R. E. 1983. *Cooperative learning.* New York: Longman.

Stahl, S. A. 1992. Saying the "p" word: Nine guidelines for exemplary phonics instruction. *The Reading Teacher* 46(1): 38–44.

Stanovitch, K. E. 1986. Mathew effects in reading: Same consequences of individual differences in the acquisition of literacy. *Reading Research Quarterly* 21(4): 360–406.

Starrett, E. V. 2000. *The mindful school: Teaching phonics for balanced reading.* Arlington Heights, IL: SkyLight Training and Publishing.

Stauffer, R. 1969. *Teaching reading as a thinking process.* New York: Harper and Row.

Sylwester, R. 1995. *A celebration of neurons: An educator's guide to the human brain.* Alexandria , VA: ASCD.

———. ed. 1999. *Student brains, school issues: A collection of articles.* Arlington Heights, IL: SkyLight Training and Publishing.

Technology Counts. 1998. [Special issue] *Education Week,* November, 1–114.

United States Department of Education. 1986. *What works: Research about teaching and learning.* Washington, D.C.: United States Department of Education.

Wisconsin Department of Education. *Strategic Learning in the Content Areas.* Madison, Wisconsin: Wisconsin Department of Education.

NOTES